WOW! LOOK AT THIS!

CW00983223

Contents

Race you to the start of the comic!

Zoooom

Super M to the Rescue!

At the supermarket with Mum ...

Bunny is lost!

Waaah!

I'm Super Mini – can I help you?

But how?

rub Rub.

I rub my magic cup ...

The End

5

Jay at the Beach

A day at the beach...

Mr Slime was there, too.

Those kids make me cross!

Stinky seaweed!

We can win this!

PRIZE
for best
Sandcastle

PRIZE
for best
Sandcastle

Hee, hee!

Zzzz

The kids got the prize.

Help!

Nip! Nip!

Fun by the Sea!

There are lots of ways to have fun by the sea!

You can play with your friends.

You can go for a swim.

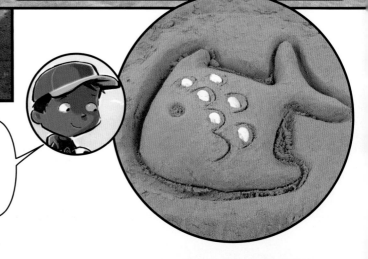

You can make cool shapes in the sand!

The Mermaids' Sleepover

Beach Jokes

Q. What sort of fish is good with ice-cream?

A. A jellyfish!

Q. What did the sea say to the mermaids?

A. Nothing. It just gave a wave!

Q. What happens when it rains cats and dogs?

A. You might step in a poodle!